# HOW TO PLAY
# VIOLIN

## Max Jaffa

Elm Tree Books
International Music Publications

Copyright © 1986 by International Music Publications

First published in Great Britain 1986
by Elm Tree Books Ltd
27 Wrights Lane, London W8 5TZ

in association with

International Music Publications
Southend Road, Woodford Green, Essex IG8 8HN

British Library Cataloguing in Publication Data
Jaffa, Max
   How to play violin. – (Elm Tree/IMP music
   reference series)
   1. Violin
   I. Title
   787.1'07'12      MT260

   ISBN 0-241-11964-2
   ISBN 0-241-11963-4 Pbk

Printed in Great Britain by
St Edmundsbury Press Ltd, Bury St Edmunds, Suffolk

# Foreword

If only I could have read Max Jaffa's book when I was a child, who knows, today I might be leading the London Symphony Orchestra.

Let me explain. At the age of nine I acquired a half-size violin, but, after struggling for weeks trying to play "The Bluebells of Scotland", I decided that Yehudi Menuhin had nothing to fear from me; so my fiddle and I agreed not to fight anymore. I still have the violin and I often look at it but I still can't believe such a little thing can make such an excruciating noise. Where were you Max when I needed you?

Maybe Max wasn't around to help me in my childhood, but he certainly helped me when I first started with the E.M.I. Record Company as a young, inexperienced, very nervous Musical Director.

On occasions I had to conduct my orchestra for recording sessions with many of the big American stars such as Howard Keel, Mel Torme, Judy Garland and numerous others. Naturally, I was scared stiff, but I was fortunate, on many of the sessions, to have Max Jaffa as my violin leader. His slow smile of encouragement as we approached and conquered a tricky passage in the orchestration was worth a thousand words. If only it were possible to print that smile, I'm sure it would work wonders for the readers of this book.

I love the way Max explains how to phrase a piece of music. To quote him:- "The fiddle player should sing through his instrument". Also, his suggestion to record oneself on cassette and listen to the play-back. It's little things like these that the student might not think of, but these are the things that make practising a pleasure instead of a chore.

You know, this book makes everything sound so easy and exciting that I'm tempted to have another go myself. So, if you can't find me for the next few days, have a look up in my loft — you'll find me up there practising.

Happy fiddling!

Geoff Love

I would like to express my everlasting gratitude to Peggy Jones and Cecil Bolton for their invaluable assistance in the preparation of this book. Without them I don't think I could have done it!!!

MAX JAFFA

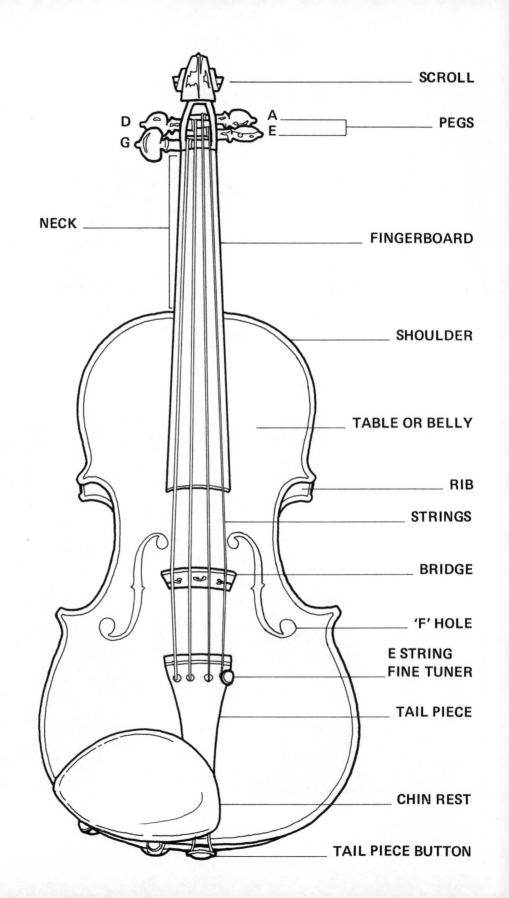

SCROLL

PEGS

D A
G E

NECK

FINGERBOARD

SHOULDER

TABLE OR BELLY

RIB

STRINGS

BRIDGE

'F' HOLE

E STRING
FINE TUNER

TAIL PIECE

CHIN REST

TAIL PIECE BUTTON

# Contents

# A little about the Violin

The 'fiddel' — or fiddle as we call it today — was an early bowed string instrument already being used in the 12th century. It was played under the chin, with the bowing hand palm downwards and with a convex bow. The bow 'fiddel' was usually flat-backed and did not have a waist as violins do today.

The violin itself emerged in the 17th century and has remained virtually unchanged since then.

The great Amati, whose pupils were Stradivarius and Guarnerius and all the great makers of the Cremonese school, made violins early in the seventeenth century and quite a few Stradivarius and Guarnerius were made before 1700 — mine was made in 1704. Today violin makers all over the world have detailed plans of how Amati, Stradivarius and Guarnerius were made. They have a template and they try to copy and they will go so far as to say, when they have made a violin to these plans, that this is a model of a Stradivarius made at such and such a date.

Although the structure of the violin has scarcely changed I think the sound today is probably better than it was. It is probably a more brilliant and carrying sound because in the seventeenth century this was not required as they did not have enormous concert halls to play in as we have today. They would play in salons and in the private houses of their patrons, or they were Court musicians, playing for Kings, Dukes etc and their entourage.

A few slight changes have been made over the years. Violins are strung differently today, the bridge has been changed, various pieces are made from different materials, the pegs and tail piece are probably a matching set and the soundpost has been slightly adjusted, because a minute adjustment of the soundpost inside the violin will change its tone and sound, and therefore makers have striven to find the right place for the soundpost. When it is in the right place you can get a uniformity of sound over all four strings, the largest, most carrying and, at the same time, the soft round tone which, together, make the violin a singing instrument. The strings have also been changed. At one time they used an E string made of silk. In fact, up to about twenty-five years ago, Jascha Heifetz still used one because it gave such a beautiful sound. However, it is not a practical proposition for people playing night after night in concerts all over the world because the silk string does not last. The other strings were made of gut, catgut as it was called. Today the E string is usually of either chrome steel or just steel and the A, D and G strings are of gut cord wound in silver and now there are some that are wound in chrome or stainless steel, but the core is gut to this day. About twenty-five years ago American makers of violins introduced a nylon string which was made of gut covered in nylon because they thought the nylon would last forever. However, these strings developed a fault very quickly. They squeaked! They did not stay true for very long and you just could not be sure that you were going to produce a note. So the nylon string was quickly abandoned and since then there have been no innovations.

The table of the violin is still mostly made of pine and the back of maple as in the days of the great makers.

An interesting point is that in the sixteenth century the violin was not considered a 'serious' instrument and lyres and viols were given all the important parts to play. But from the beginning of the seventeenth century the violin took over and by the end of the century had completely displaced the viol, by virtue of its brilliant tone and power.

# Buying or hiring?

Nowadays you can hire an instrument or hire with the option to buy which we could never do in my day, as a student.

If you are wanting to buy a fiddle and you don't know exactly how to go about it, the best way perhaps is to go to a sale. Now there are sales held regularly at Sothebys, Christies, Phillips etc in London and they do hold them in other parts of the country as well. Prior to the day of the sale, you should get a catalogue and go to the showroom and all the instruments will be there for you to look at, pick up and actually try. You can also, in some cases, get an estimated price, but the point is that you can go along and try a hundred if you wish to, and take somebody with you who knows about the instruments. Some of them may not be fully strung but there will be plenty there that are. I have been to many sales and you will see all sorts of people from young students to old age pensioners playing on the instruments, trying them out, listening to them.

You must first of all make up your mind that you are going to continue playing the violin and not just do it for a year or two. Somebody who is serious about playing the violin, wants to play and wants to play fairly decently, I would say, their best bet is to buy — if they can afford to. You will, of course, know roughly how much you can afford to pay and if you buy anything halfway decent it will certainly appreciate in value over the years. So from an investment point of view you will be alright. All classical stringed instruments appreciate in value, with age.

If you see an instrument you particularly like ask a member of the staff — there will always be a number of them around the room — if they would tell you how much the instrument might fetch. After marking it in your catalogue, you go along to the sale room on the day of the sale and when it comes up, you bid for it and, hopefully, you get it.

In a sale the prices may start at about £100, if the fiddle was not worth that it would not be put in the sale. At £100 it would not be a marvellous instrument, but it would serve to start with and later, when you have decided that you are going to play seriously, and for the rest of your life, you can change to a better instrument.

To buy an instrument which will give pleasure to play and would also be a good investment you would need to pay at least £1,000.

I would recommend that a child starting to play should go to a reputable dealer — again taking somebody with you who knows about violins. These dealers supply schools with instruments and they are very fair and know what is needed. They will advise the size of an instrument on which to start. For instance a small child would require a quarter size instrument, older children a half or three-quarter until they can cope with a full size instrument. They will also put a fiddle in good working order. It is not worth buying a cheap fiddle in a sale thinking you can get a dealer and repairer to put it into good shape for you, as this can cost you quite a lot of money.

# The Bow

The bow is very important indeed, it can be worth almost as much as the fiddle. You can buy a brand-new bow from a dealer which need not cost a lot — say about £50 or something like that. A gold-mounted bow made by a reputable maker could be worth about £2,000 and it might have cost only £5 or even less originally — again a worthwhile investment for the dedicated student.

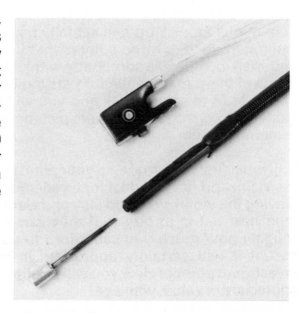

The tension of the bow hair is controlled by a screw in the nut of the bow. (See illustration below). This can be made of ebony, but in the more expensive bows can be made of tortoiseshell or ivory, adorned with inlaid mother-of-pearl. I myself have a silver one and a gold one, but I have been playing for many years and can perhaps be allowed to indulge myself. Anyway, from the nut there is a long thin screw which goes into the nut of the bow and above this is where you hold. The nut sticks out a bit from your fingers. The screw goes into the wood of the bow which has been bored to take it, and that goes through the little nut.

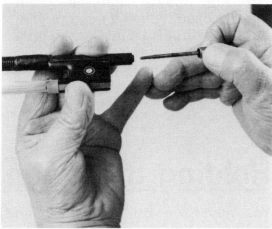

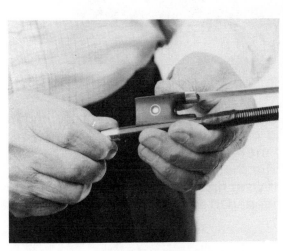

Just tighten this to get the correct tension of the bow. Here again some people like to play with a very tight bow and some people like to play with less tension on the bow hair. Fritz Kreisler played with a very tight bow and the stick was practically straight, there was no slight curve and the hair was quite a distance from this straight bow whereas, in most cases, the bow retains a slight natural curve and the bow hair is straight and taut. Nobody, of course, plays with an absolutely flat bow. You would get no sound at all! Which maybe the neighbours would like, but you would not.

The bow hair, of course, needs rosin. This you buy from your dealer, it is the solid residue left after turpentine has been distilled and you don't have to put on a lot, but what you do need to do is to put enough on so that you can draw the bow across the strings with a certain amount of pressure that will give you a note. If there is no rosin on the bow at all it will just float over the top of the strings, it is the rosin which grips that part of the string that you are bowing on to produce a note.

You should put rosin on your bow every time you play — just a couple of rubs of rosin should be sufficient.

When you have a bow re-haired or when you buy a new one from a dealer, he will rosin the bow for you in its initial stage with its brand-new untouched hair. When you get the bow first and the hair has been already used, you will need to give it three or four rubs full-length on a piece of rosin, almost like 'playing' the piece of rosin.

# Holding the Violin

You must have your violin firmly and comfortably placed between your chin and your shoulder, with your left hand on the neck of the violin and your thumb in the proper position, which is more or less at a right angle to your second finger in the first position. But the most important thing is that your left arm must be under the violin so that your fingers come straight down on to the string with the strength which is needed to sustain the note. The fingers should not come down at an angle.

I have noticed that a lot of students today have not been shown, what I consider to be, the correct way to hold the violin and they then have difficulties because they have not got their left arm in the correct position.

The correct way is not the most comfortable position but with practice it will become the most natural way to hold your violin, and the more under the violin you can get your left elbow, across what will be the back of the violin, the more at right angles your fingers will come down on the strings.

I would also mention, in passing, that I do not think people should play with a wrist watch on or a ring on any finger of the hand, as I feel this is a hindrance.

Everybody has different sized hands and fingers, some are very weak and when you put your fingers down they have got to be put down on the string with strength. The strings are raised from the fingerboard to a uniform height suitable for most players but in some cases, because of the formation of the players hands and fingers, the strings above the fingerboard, where they stretch from the pegs across the bridge, can be made higher or lower by the height of the bridge, and this can be adjusted to suit by your dealer. The fingers must be put down so that the string is 'hit' by the tip of the finger and pressed down on to the fingerboard and your fingers must be strong enough to hold that note down for the full length of the bow or however long the note is that you are playing and in some cases that can be quite a long time. If you take what is, just to look at a simple piece of music well known to all aspiring violinists — the AIR ON A G STRING.

Now, the G string is the lowest and the tension on it is probably greater than the tension on the other strings and the very first note sounds for nine beats, and that note has got to be held in one bow with the fingers pressed down, and that is quite a long time, so this is a marvellous piece to actually practise on. Of course you do not need this piece, all you need is an ordinary scale, but you must play each note as long as you comfortably can with the bow and throughout the finger has to be strong on the string.

You should play on each string separately and by doing this you will cover another sort of attitude and that is the change in the bow from one string to another so that in fact you are combining the whole length of the bow, the strength of the fingers and changing from one string to another, so you have three practices in one.

The bow is held in the right hand with the bent thumb between the frog, or nut, and the stick. The four fingers placed on to the stick as they would naturally fall, as you will see in the accompanying illustration.

To increase the volume of tone, pressure is increased on the bow stick by the fore-finger.

# Chin-rests (and shoulder pads)

There are very many types of chin-rest nowadays, but before I talk about them I would just like to say a word about shoulder-pads. I do not agree with the use of these at all. In some cases this is just a pad — old fashioned ones used to be covered in velvet. It is not really a pad, more like a little cushion which was either made for the player or bought from a shop which would have them in all sorts of shapes and sizes. The pad is fitted on to the tail piece button by a 'keyhole shaped' piece of leather at the other end.

Today they have something which I call a 'Bailey Bridge'. This is a contraption which fits across under the violin and rests across the shoulder and is clipped on to both edges of the violin. It is very much used today and there is one type designed by Yehudi Menuhin which is used by all his pupils. But, I feel this is quite a large piece of equipment to fit under a beautiful violin and I don't like it. I have never used one nor did my teacher or his teacher before him because they felt that the use of anything like this dampens the sound as it interferes with the natural vibration of the violin. The wood vibrates and if you put something solid up against it, it cannot vibrate and it can act, in some cases, as a sort of mute.

So, on to chin-rests. You have to find the right sort of chin-rest for yourself and in my opinion if a student is using a pad and a chin-rest he needs the pad because he has the wrong sort of chin-rest. The violin should not really be gripped between the chin and the shoulder. It has to be fairly firm, of course, to allow it to stay put when your hand is moving up and down the instrument in various positions.

Very often one buys a violin which already has a chin-rest on it and if you buy from a dealer he will change it for you to something more suitable. He will show you what he has and you can try them out. It only takes a minute to take one chin-rest off and put another one on. They are only screwed or clamped on and they do not harm the violin because they are only on the very edge of it. The chin-rest itself does not touch the violin. It is suspended from it, not like the pads which in some cases cover quite a large piece of the violin.

# The Strings

You will quickly learn the difference in the strings because they are not evenly spaced, simply because of the curvature of the fingerboard. If the strings were absolutely level you would be playing on two strings at the same time and somebody just learning may not realise this. You would just look at a fiddle and think there was just a fingerboard and four strings and it would not occur to you, quite rightly I think, that the strings are not evenly spread.

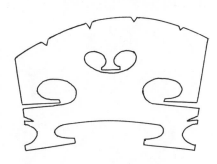

There is a slight change and difference and this is made possible by the little notches that are cut in the bridge to take the string from the peg up the fingerboard over the bridge. The strings have got to stay on the bridge and in order to do so the bridge has these four little notches in it.

# Tuning

In order to tune the violin you must be given a true note, in some form or other. At one time one went to the piano, struck the A or a D minor triad (chord) and tuned from there. However, now, if you have one of the electronic tuners, which are not expensive, you get this electronic note and tune the A string. You always tune the A first, that is traditional.

I can't tell you why except that if you are playing with an orchestra the oboist always gives the A. So, you tune your A string to the pitch that is correct and from there you can tune the other strings, a fifth apart. You tune the G, and the D, and the E last because that requires a very minute adjustement AND FOR THIS you have got a fine adjuster which is fixed to the tail piece. You can tune the E string very very gently which you cannot do with the pegs.

As for turning the pegs, it depends how you are holding the fiddle when you turn them. Everybody has their own way but many violinists hold the instrument between the legs, with the body of the instrument clutched between the knees and the fingerboard and strings facing them. In this way the pegs are in front of you. Turn the peg away from you, or clockwise, to make the note sharper and turn it anti-clockwise to flatten the note. Adjust the pegs and pluck the string with the thumb until you have got it right. You should not need to do much turning unless you have got a new string, when you should turn the peg gently and slowly until you reach the required pitch.

By turning the pegs you'll get the violin fairly well in tune, but in order to get the absolute fine tuning, you'll need to hold the violin in the playing position with the bow in the playing position and you use the fingers of the left hand to turn the pegs while using the bow, which of course you can't do when you are holding the violin between your knees. Just keep it in a safely held position and eventually the only way you'll tune the fiddle is in the playing position.

# Holding the Violin and Bow

I myself did not play the violin at all for a number of lessons. I was first being taught to read music without the violin, and then where those notes are on the manuscript of the music and where the notes are on the violin. But today, with all modern aids such as cassette recorders, I think it is much easier to combine the two right from the beginning.

As well as having your cassette recorder beside you, you should try to stand in front of a long mirror so that you can watch yourself playing — a kind of Do-It-Yourself teaching. Your bow must be kept central between the end of the fingerboard and the bridge and you want the bow to come down the middle and not to go from side to side and the only way to do that is to see what you are doing and the only way to see what you are doing is to stand in front of *that* mirror.

It may seem extraordinary to stand there watching yourself, but by watching yourself you'll get into the habit of playing in the right position — slowly, slowly, — it takes a lot of time and a lot of practice but eventually you'll automatically develop the habit of being able to bow in the centre and keeping the bow straight. It must not waver going up or going down.

That bow must stay right in the middle. The only time it wavers is if you want to increase tone, when you play nearer the bridge. If you want to decrease tone you play nearer the fingerboard.

You'll also need a music-stand. These are readily available from music stores. They are made of light metal and are adaptable for height and rake and collapsible.

Before we go any further, we'll take a little time learning to read music.

# Reading Music

A note is determined by its position (on and in between the five lines which make up the Music Stave). When playing the violin only the TREBLE CLEF is used i.e.

and as you can see the notes follow each other, line, space, line, space, etc. line, space, line, etc.

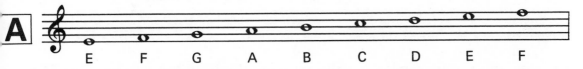

**A**    E   F   G   A   B   C   D   E   F

There are extra invisible lines which are above and below the five lines, and are only used when required, these are called LEDGER LINES.

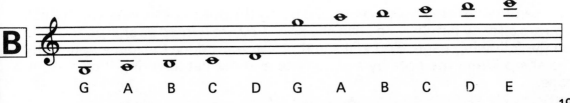

**B**    G   A   B   C   D   G   A   B   C   D   E

The names of the notes and their relation to the fingerboard can be learnt easily by studying the Position Chart on pages 98 and 99.

To raise a note to the next one higher, a sharp sign ♯ is used, and to lower it a flat ♭ is used

These are called accidentals. In some music a ♯ or ♭ will be seen after the Clef.

written                                    played

These are called 'KEY SIGNATURES': this means that all F's in the piece are read as F♯'s, similarly if a ♭ is shown.

It will be seen that all B's are flattened.

If F or B is required a natural ♮ sign is used. This 'naturalises' the note sharpened or flattened by the key signatures and remains active for the whole bar. Similarly extra ♯'s and ♭'s can be added.

naturalised    remains ♮    added ♯        ♯ again    added ♭
                            accidentals              accidental

Having been introduced to sharps and flats you'll realise that all the notes are not on example A and B on page 19.

Music is said to be measured in Octaves, this is as the name implies, an interval of eight notes.

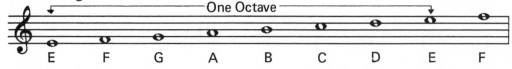

However, the distance between the notes making up the scale varies. The smallest distance between any two notes is called a Semi-tone (or Half Tone). Two semi-tones making a tone.

The semi-tones are shown on music using the sharps and flats with which you are already familiar. You can see how they are named as sharps and flats on the following page. You will see that some produce the same sound. By the sharp lifting the note by a semi-tone and the flat lowering it by a semi-tone.

Below you'll see examples A and B on page 19 combined, and below that, all the extra notes filled in.

Notes shown ♯♪ ♭♪ sound the same, although you will find they can be fingered differently.

# Positions

The violin is an instrument which is played by hand positions, any of which makes available to the player's fingers more than two octaves (24 notes) across the four strings, without moving the hand. We'll concentrate mainly on the two most popular positions, the First and Third.

In these two positions you can play in all the most popular keys and cover the most popular notes on the instrument, which will enable you to play quite a large and varied selection of melodies, see Tunes To Play, page 53. And, Your First Repertoire page 77.

Once these two positions have been learned, you'll be able to find the other positions easily with the aid of the Position Chart on page 98 and put them into practice with the scale exercises on page 65. You'll find that as you progress higher up the fingerboard, that the distance between the notes get closer together. This is best demonstrated by looking at the frets on the neck of the guitar.

When reading violin music the positions are never indicated, the correct position will be found by the fingering on the music. For instance, the A on the D string.

If played with the first finger, would put the hand in the fourth position.
If played with the second finger, would put the hand in the third position.
If played with the third finger, would put the hand in the second position.
If played with the fourth finger, would put the hand in the first position.

Again look at the Position Chart on pages 98 and 99.

The violin not being fretted (i.e. the notes being marked on the fingerboard as on a guitar), all positions have to be found by the movement of the left hand changing to the various positions, and by experience. However, this is not too difficult and with the aid of the following pictures and diagrams you'll soon become proficient in the first position.

The diagrams are marked out in semi-tones and the position of the notes are filled in. You will soon become aware of the difference in distance between a tone and a semi-tone.

These intervals are clearly shown on the fingerboard plans and the following pictures.

| Semitone | Tone |
| --- | --- |

Of course you will never put two fingers down on one string during normal playing (it does however occur when playing harmonics — this will be dealt with later in the book) and are shown here only to give a visual illustration of the difference in the interval between a tone and a semi-tone.

# The First Position

Below is a fingerboard plan of all the notes possible with the hand in the first position. Each stave of music showing the notes possible on that particular string, along with the note names and alternatives.

| E | E Open 0 | F 1 | F♯/G♭ 1  2 | G 2 | G♯/A♭ 2  3 | A 3 | A♯/B♭ 3  4 | B 4 |
|---|---|---|---|---|---|---|---|---|
| A | A Open 0 | A♯/B♭ 1  1 | B 1 | C 2 | C♯/D♭ 2  3 | D 3 | D♯/E♭ 3  4 | E 4 |
| D | D Open 0 | D♯/E♭ 1  1 | E 1 | F 2 | F♯/G♭ 2  3 | G 3 | G♯/A♭ 3  4 | A 4 |
| G | G Open 0 | G♯ A♭ 1  1 | A 1 | A♯ B♭ 1  2 | B 2 | C 3 | C♯/D♭ 3  4 | D 4 |

The four strings when tuned and played without a finger stopping the strings are known as 'open' strings and sound G, D, A and E, shown on or below the music stave as:—

When fingering is indicated the open strings are shown as O

## The scale plan of G

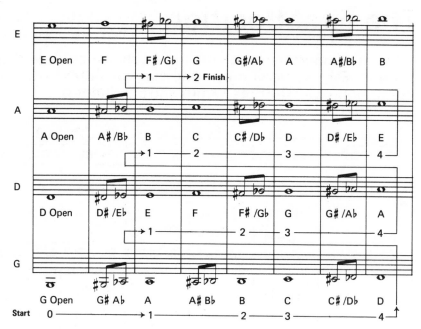

You start by fingering the first five notes on the G String (The fourth string). The first note is the G String played Open (O).

the first finger will produce A, the second finger will produce B, the third finger will produce C, the fourth finger will produce D.

G String — 4th String

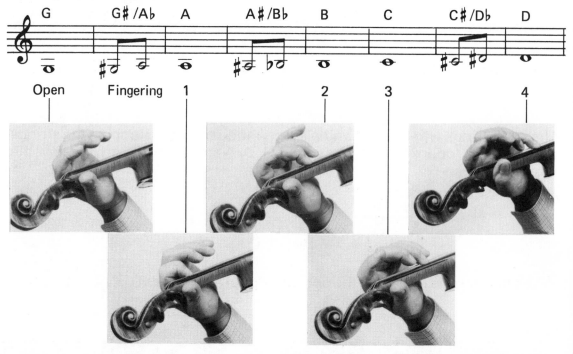

You will note that this last note is the same as the third string played open.

Now continue and start again on the third string (the D string):

the first finger will produce E, the second finger will produce F sharp (#), the third finger will produce G, the fourth finger will produce A.

Again the fourth finger on A is the same note produced by the open second or A string.

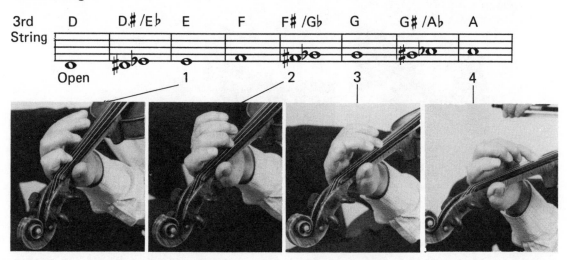

Move to the second string (the A string) and repeat in the same sequence as previously on the other strings:

the first finger will produce B, the second finger will produce C, the third finger will produce D, the fourth finger will produce E.

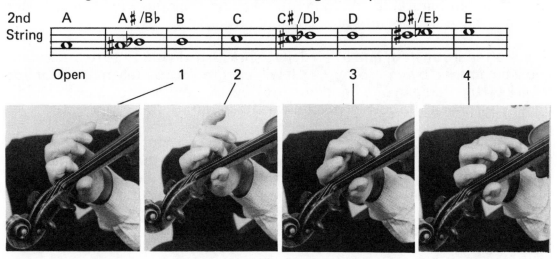

Again the fourth finger will produce the same note as the open first string or E string.

Do the same on the first string, (the E string):

The first finger will produce F sharp, the second finger will produce G. This completes the fingering for the scale of G.

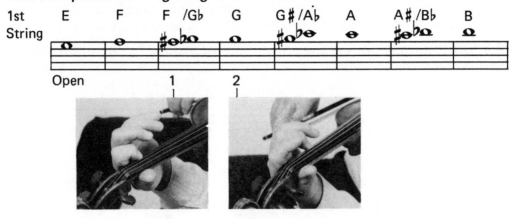

# Practise

To practise properly you should not play constantly for more than 45 minutes at a time, take a rest for 10 minutes or so, practise for another 45 minutes. I myself used to practice for eight hours a day when I first began studying but, of course, I was not playing for the whole of that time. Playing the violin is very tiring, especially for a new young player, and you should stop the moment you feel tired. In playing the hands and arms are held in a position which it is not natural for the body to take and they have to remain in this position – have another look at the picture on page 14.

If you can spare an hour and a half daily to practise, divided into two sessions, you'll be amazed by your progress. It will become absolutely natural for you to pick up the fiddle in one hand and the bow in the other, to place the fiddle under your chin in the correct position and to begin.

Once ready to practise you must know what to practise and the best thing to do, dull as it may seem and horrid as it may sound at the beginning to your family, and perhaps the neighbours, is to play scales. You must do this so that you learn where the notes are and how to play them in tune, and nowadays learning to play in tune is so much easier than it was when I began. The best thing to do is to place a small cassette recorder near you, to switch it on and play a scale. You can then play the recording back and hear just how well — or badly — you are playing your scales. You can then correct your mistakes and you will soon start to play in tune. By this method you attune your ear and learn to listen.

Your ear will help you to pitch the notes as you finger them on the instrument.

Quite early on you'll realise that the notes you are playing on the instrument will not necessarily be in tune just by you putting down one finger after the next. You'll have to adjust the intonation to make sure you have got the correct interval.

All this sounds very complicated, but it isn't really because all you need to do is to use your 'ear' when playing these notes and you'll quickly realise that you are not playing the right note and you compensate for that.

Now, after having done all these slightly complicated manoeuvres on the fiddle you have, in fact, learned the difference between your fingers coming down and producing a semi-tone or a full tone and we'll assume that your ear has told you that you have done this. So — congratulations, you have now completed your first scale without actually playing it.

# Beginning to Play

The violin is one of the most difficult instruments to play because there are so many things to be taken into consideration. You have to put your fingers in the right place with no help at all from any of the parts of the violin. Pressure is exerted by the fingers holding the bow and usually with the index finger of the right hand pressing down slightly, but different violinists use different fingers of the right hand, some lift the little finger off the bow, others lift the first finger off.

If the bow is not absolutely straight you may get a whistle. Particularly on open strings, because there is a natural harmonic that can sound if the bow is not playing on that string in the absolute right position and with the right pressure.

# The Scale of G (First Position)

So we'll begin to play on one string. Let us say you begin on the G string, starting to play a scale of G major and you play the open G and the first finger that goes down is A, the second finger is B, the third finger goes down and that is C. Now, for the next note which is D you can do one of two things. you can either put down the fourth finger on the G string or you can go on to the next string, the open D. The best thing I would suggest is to use the fourth finger because that is the weakest finger and the more you use it the stronger it will become, and the open D string may not be absolutely in tune. And then, of course, you must remember the distance between one finger and another changes because between the open G string and the first finger, well, that's fine because you learn where that is, and the next note, the B, is a full tone, but the next note to the B, the C, is only half a tone so the third finger coming down following the second is closer than the second finger following the first. And the third finger having played the C you then want to go on to the D with the fourth finger, still on the G string. This is a whole tone (equivalent to two semitones) so the distance between these two notes is greater than between the two previous notes. Refer back to the pictures on pages 22 to 26.

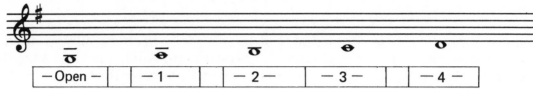

Play each note as a separate long note. Use the full length of the bow keeping it central and with the same pressure.

The same (as for G string) applies for the D string.

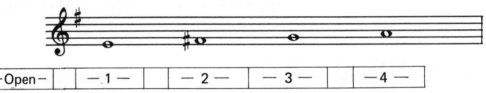

Then for A string.

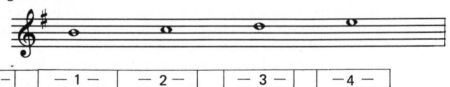

Then for E string.

# Bowing

An 'up bow' indicates that you start at the tip of the bow and push the bow up until you come to the nut. A 'down bow' is starting at the nut of the bow and the bow travelling downwards to the tip. Or, of course, you would use shorter or longer bow strokes as is necessary to play the piece in the correct tempo.

Bowing is usually shown on violin music by a slur over the notes to be played in one bow.

The direction is indicated by the two signs.

Up Bow                                    Down Bow

Unless otherwise indicated proceed with alternate up and down bowing, after starting in the direction indicated on the first note.

As you become more proficient you may decide that a particular piece of music might sound better if you adapt the bowing signs to suit your own sense of phrasing.

Now Try The Scale Of G Complete.

Scale up — one note to a bow.

Scale down

After the scale practice you can progress to the arpeggios, in the same (first) position. Here you will eventually learn to cross the strings in one bow without making any difference in tone. The fingers will change but you play an arpeggio across all the four strings and you can do that first with all detached long bows and then eventually legato (slurred) — maybe three or four notes to a bow. You should learn the scale of G first and then do the arpeggio. Play the first four notes and go on to the next octave still in the first position. In arpeggios it is much easier and safer intonationwise to use the open strings unless you are playing one in a slow piece of music where it sounds better if you don't use the open strings, to be sure of being in tune.

Here It Is written in Music Notation.

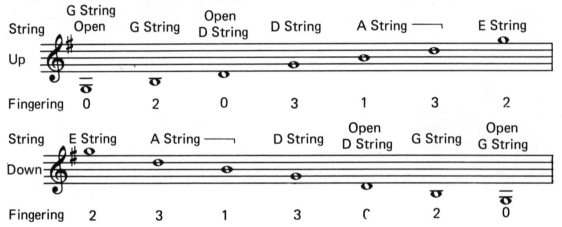

## The Arpeggio Plan of G

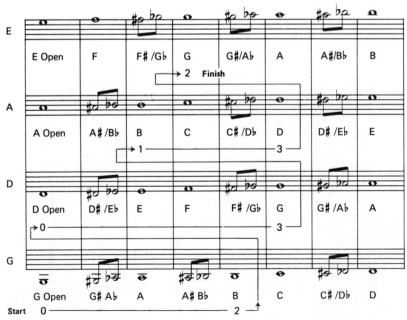

You can now play the scale of G and the arpeggio, and I think it is better to do this rather than to try a simple tune after the scale. You have, by doing the scale and arpeggio of G in long and short bows, begun to get the 'feel' of playing the violin.

Having learned to play in the first position the scale of G and the arpeggio for G, go on to the next, starting with the first finger on the G string, which is A. You are now going to play the scale of A again over the two octaves in the first position.

## The Scale Of A

### The Scale Up

### The Scale Down

### The Scale Plan Of A

Here is the arpeggio of A up and down.

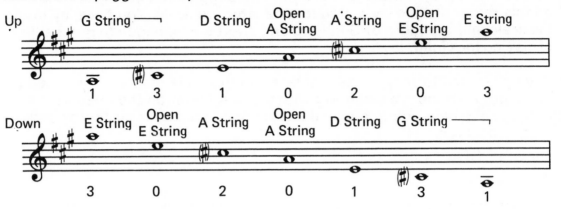

The Arpeggio Plan Of A

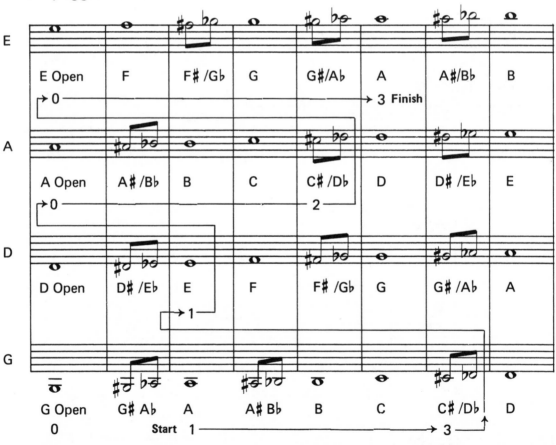

You can do one more scale in the first position. This is a more difficult one, B major, having five sharps and is only included here to complete the first position. This key is popular with proficient players.

# The Scale of B

## The Scale Plan of B

## The Arpeggio of B

*Here we have to use the same finger for two notes. Play the first note in the normal way and then move the finger quickly to the next note.

33

## The Arpeggio Plan of B

The practice of scales and arpeggios is the best way to learn positions and notation. The scales and arpeggios you are most likely to come across are on page 65. You will also see minor scales. Because of their unusual construction, sharps, flats and sometimes naturals need to be added. I have used the scale known as the Melodic Minor.

# Major and Minor Scales

Compare the different structure of the Major Scale of C and its relative A Minor shown below:

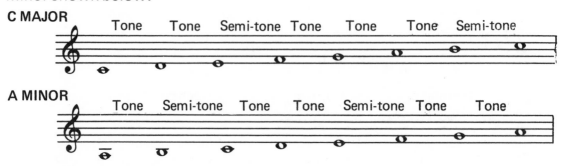

*Minor Scales are given in the Scale Section starting on page 65.*

The Scale Plan of A minor (All notes First Position)

# Note values

The length of each note is decided by its appearance.

The most common basic value used is a CROTCHET ♩ This can be divided into two QUAVERS ♪♪ (or ♫) 4 SEMI-QUAVERS ♬♬ (♬♬ or ♬♬) two CROTCHETS also make a MINIM ♩, and 2 MINIMS makes a SEMI-BREVE. o

The following table will explain how these values are arrived at in a bar of 4 crotchets in a bar.

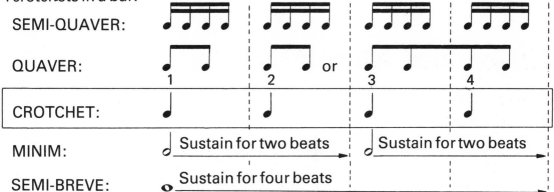

Quavers and Semi-quavers can be grouped in several combinations, with each group in value to one Crotchet, e.g.

Sometimes a beat is divided into 3 (triplets) by joining notes in the following way:-

3 QUAVERS with a figure 3 over the top, i.e. ♪♪♪ equals one CROTCHET ♩

3 CROTCHETS ♩ ♩ ♩ likewise equals a MINIM ♩

3 MINIMS ♩ ♩ ♩ equal a SEMI-BREVE o

The following table will show how they are spread over a bar of 4 CROTCHETS

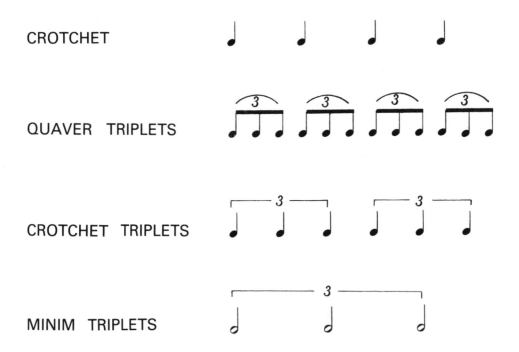

CROTCHET

QUAVER TRIPLETS

CROTCHET TRIPLETS

MINIM TRIPLETS

A dot after any note increases its value by half.

♪. = ♪ Tied to ♪     ♩. = ♩ Tied to ♩

♩. = ♩ Tied to ♪     o· = o Tied to ♩

The curved lines in the examples above are called tie-lines. They indicate that both notes are held for their collective value.

At the beginning of all music there is a sign called a CLEF. In violin music only the TREBLE-CLEF is used ( 𝄞 ), and next to that there are two figures, one above the other, e.g. $\frac{4}{4}$. The top figure denotes the value of the beat.

A CROTCHET is shown as 4, so that four CROTCHETS in a bar shown as $\frac{4}{4}$, and 3 CROTCHETS as $\frac{3}{4}$.

A MINIM is shown as 2, so 2 MINIMS in a bar are shown as $\frac{2}{2}$.

A QUAVER is shown as 8, so 6 QUAVERS in a bar are shown as $\frac{6}{8}$.

Below you will find a few of the ways notes can be grouped into bars.

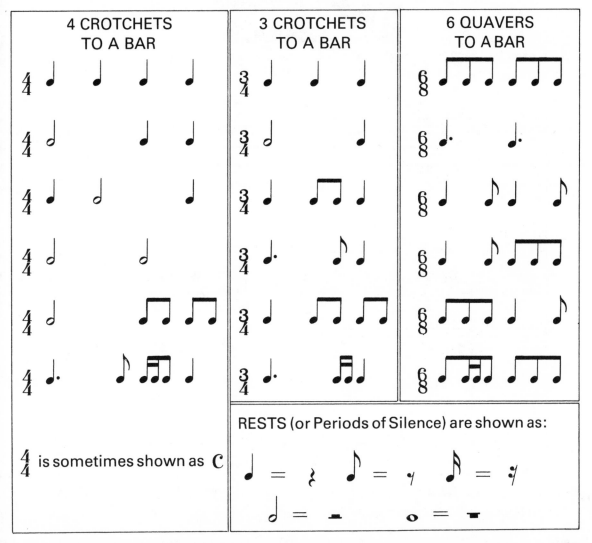

$\frac{4}{4}$ is sometimes shown as **C**

# The Third Position

After the first position the most difficult position is the second. Other than for the few odd notes you might come across in a piece of music, this is seldom used. If possible, not at all, because the intonation in the second position is very tricky and you'll find even experienced violinists will fight shy of this position.

So we will go on to the Third Position, which starts on C on the G string.

All Notes In The Third Position.

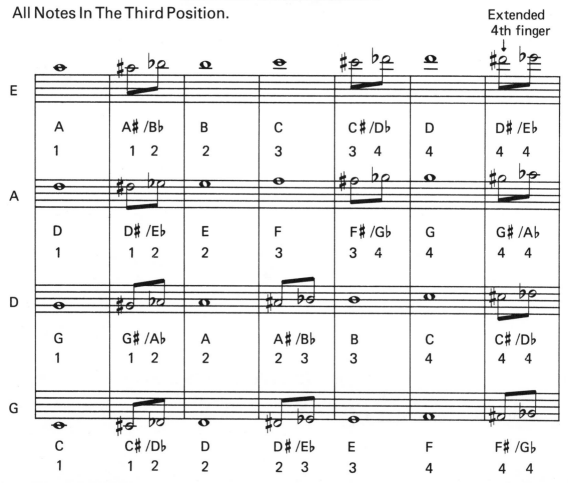

Practise by playing the scales in their various positions, then you get to the point where by playing your scales and arpeggios you learn exactly where a note is on the fiddle, and then you can put your finger straight down on that note because you *do* know where it is.

Sometimes a piece of music will start on a fairly high note, perhaps in one of the positions that is not normally practiced in. You must know, without having to pluck the note quietly to yourself to find out if you are on the right note, that you can put your finger on the right position. This comes with practice.

Here is the Scale C

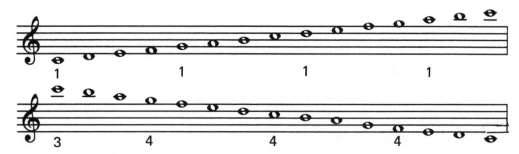

The Scale Plan Of C. All Notes In Third Position.

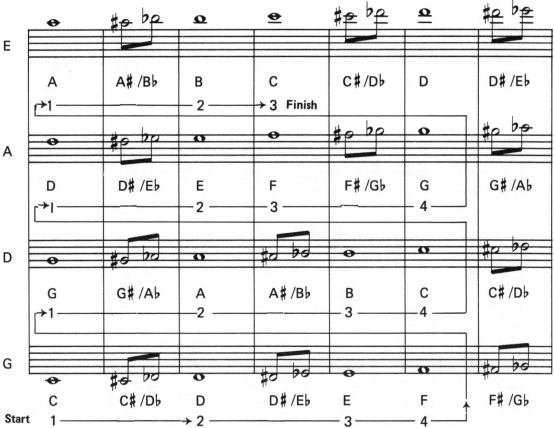

## The Arpeggio of C

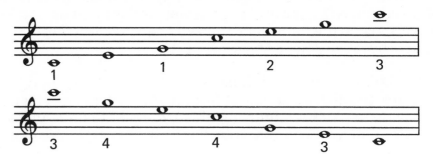

## The Arpeggio Plan of C. All Notes In Third Position.

## The Scale Of D

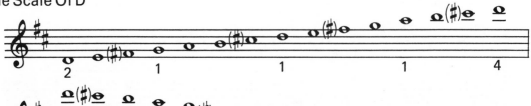

40

## The Scale Plan Of D. All Notes In Third Position.

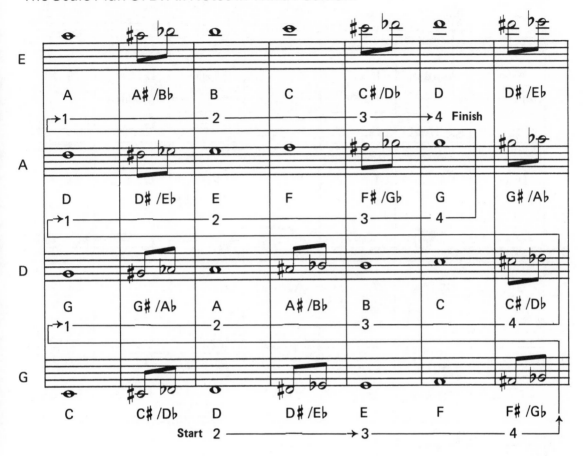

## The Arpeggio Of D

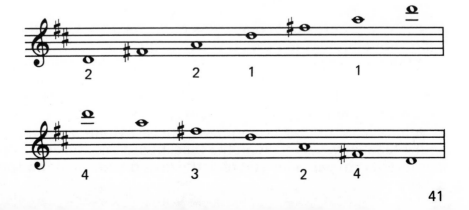

**The Arpeggio Plan of D. All Notes In Third Position.**

# More About Bowing

Having learnt all this you can now start to learn to play two notes to a bow. In other words, you join up the first two notes of the scale. So you'll start on the open G string and allow half a bow on that, and then put the first finger down to play the A with the second half of the bow in the same stroke. So that you then play what we call legato, slurred in a succession of notes — and go on doing this up the scale.

And so you progress and play three notes next time. But the most important thing about this — and now you have begun you really must be very diligent about this — is to do it so often that the actual holding of the violin and the putting of the bow on the string and the drawing of the bow, becomes second nature to you. It is very like a child learning to write. He has never written before, never held a pencil and never sat before a sheet of blank paper — just as you have, at the beginning, never held a violin or read a piece of music. So the teacher writes an A on the blackboard and the child attempts to copy it on its sheet of paper, as you read the note on the music and attempt to make it on your violin. It will not be a very good 'A' or a very good note to start with, but soon it will be better and you progress to the next letter — or note. Soon you will be making separate notes, as the child makes separate letters, perfectly. And then comes the pleasure of joining up letters to make 'real' writing or playing a succession of notes to make 'real' music. It really is very similar.

* Play The Scale Of G Again — This Time Bowed — Two or Three Notes To The Bow.

Two Notes to a Bow

Three Notes to a Bow

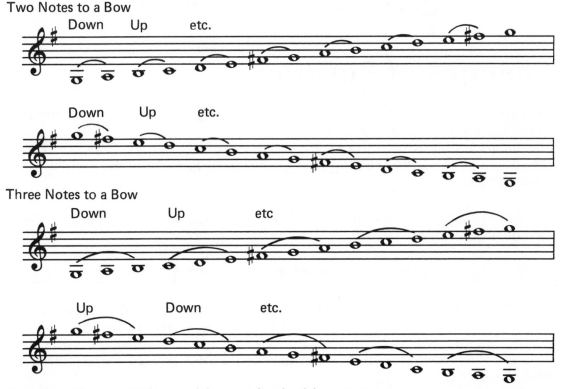

Practice all your scales and Arpeggios in this manner.

* You will find the bowing marked for you in the sections Tunes To Play, and Your First Repertoire.

Now we have come to the method used when bowing repeated notes. To play quick repeated notes known as Spiccato usually written as Spicc. The bow bounces slightly off the string between each note, no matter how fast. Kreisler liked to have his bow very tight but most players like to have a little sort of give. But, there again, the student may find that he or she can produce spiccato bowing better by slightly tightening the tension of the bow.

Repeated notes are usually played in separate bows, but once you have mastered the spiccato playing you'll be able to use this technique to detach repeated notes, played in the same bow.

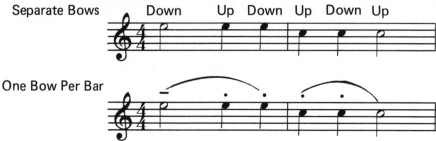

# Changes of Position

One goes from first position to third on one string and then changes position from first to third over two strings.

For instance play B with the second finger on the G String then cross to G (Third Position) on the D String using the first finger. Move the hand and try not to slide the finger.

In passing from one position to another you must take great care that this change is inaudible.

You have to change position on the E string to get higher notes.

It is not necessary to go very much higher on the D, A and E strings when you are learning, although later, when you are playing a piece, you may find it sounds nicer to play higher up on the D string or the A string rather than go on to the E string. It might suit the music better and give you a different tone colour.

To conclude this section — always remember that playing the fiddle itself is the very best way to learn. Find your way around the fiddle and at the same time, strengthen your arms and fingers.

Try playing some more tunes, starting on page 53 & 77

# Vibrato

There are two methods for using vibrato on a note, which is usually a fairly long note. (In fact, there are three methods, but one that should never be used is by bending the wrist to and fro very quickly). So — there are two proper forms. One is a finger vibrato where it is just the finger that is bent playing the note, moving backwards and forwards. But, of course, the finger on the string must never change position or you'll get another note. The other method is when the whole forearm, the hand and the finger move as one. The most important thing about vibrato, which is something that will eventually come naturally to the player is that the note that is being vibrated

is held by having a finger on the string, and being bent backwards and forwards, thus vibrating the note. Or you can, as I said, use the whole forearm, from the elbow down to the finger-tip.

# Tremolo

Tremolo is used almost only in orchestral playing, when the bow is moved very swiftly up and down on a certain note or succession of notes. Usually you tremolo on one note and then, after a certain time, you might need to change the note, but continue the tremolo. The bow is moved a very short distance and very quickly up and down and a whole section doing this causes the tremolo sound. It is purely sound effect and rarely encountered in solo playing and is written

# Trill

A trill is played mainly between two notes which are next to each other. Let us say you want a trill with an E or an F in any position — you do that by holding down one note which is usually the bottom note and moving the finger which is playing the next note on and off the string very quickly and is written

# Phrasing

Phrasing is a very personal thing. If one is playing a transcription or an arrangement of a well-known song, obviously the best way to phrase it would be as if you yourself were singing that song, but instead of singing you are playing it on the violin. Or, you can listen to a recording of somebody singing and copy their phrasing. What you must do is make the violin sing. Fritz Kreisler was the greatest master at making the violin sing and luckily there are still recordings of him which we can listen to. A short discography is given on page 94.

If you are playing with an orchestra, the leader (the principal violin) will actually mark the bowing of the piece you are playing and everybody will copy into their part his bowing and he, having talked to the conductor, will be responsible for phrasing as the conductor wishes. He will then communicate this to the string section so that you all work together.

For the soloist however phrasing is purely a personal thing. The golden rule is that it should sound very pleasant to the ear and should not deviate from the normal rhythm of the piece you are playing. You must keep within the bounds of the tempo marked. The most beautiful phrasing comes purely from nuance. But, you must always think of singing. The violin is a singing instrument, not a percussive one and the fiddle player should sing through his instrument.

Two More Scales and Arpeggios. E and F.

To play the Scale of E start with the second finger on E on the G string – this gives you the fourth position (IV) — SEE POSITION CHART.

The Scale of E

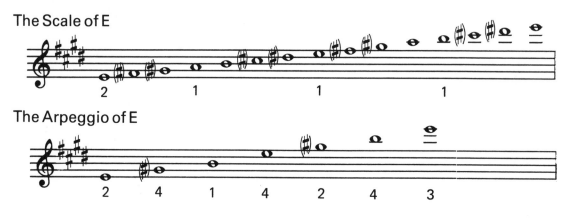

The Arpeggio of E

To play the scale of F, start with the second finger on the F on the G string. This will give you the fifth position (V).

The Scale of F

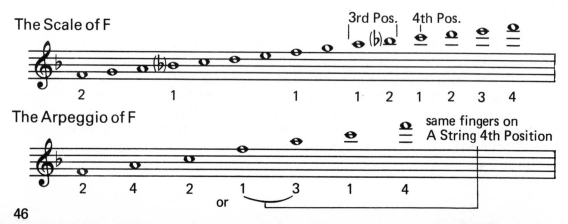

The Arpeggio of F

# Chromatic Scales

Chromatic Scales are when you play in semi-tones and there are various ways of fingering these.

Using the old fashioned method you started on the open string and then put down the first finger — say you started on the G and put the first finger down on the G sharp, the first finger then slides to the A natural. The second finger plays the A sharp and slides to the B natural. The C is then played with the third finger, the C sharp is played with the fourth finger... and so on. The sliding finger has to be beautifully done so that it cannot be heard. If you play a slow slurred legato chromatic then you would probably hear it. If you played quickly as in the "FLIGHT OF THE BUMBLEBEE", it would be inaudible. You have to detach the bow for each note anyway and you can use the same finger twice. But, in the last few years a different fingering has been developed where you change without using a sliding finger and I would advocate using this method.

The Chromatic Scale can start on any note.

# Pizzicato

Having in front of you the pizzicato notes that you are going to play, the first thing to do is to select the first note with the fingers of the left hand. To pluck the strings you use the first finger of the right hand, generally holding the bow, because very often you get a few bars of pizzicato and then almost immediately go back to the bow. You hold the fingers of the left hand down stopping the note that you are going to play and then you pluck that string just at the top of the fingerboard, (not in the space between the bridge and the fingerboard). The first finger of the right hand still holding the bow.

There are, of course, whole pieces which are purely pizzicato, such as the Strauss "Pizzicato Polka", Leroy Anderson's "Plink, Plank, Plunk" and "Sylvia". Some of these pieces can be found on pages 86 and 87. These are fun to play and if you do it the right way can sound very pleasant and different.

There is another way of playing pizzicato, in a sort of guitar style. For playing a whole piece in pizzicato you can put your fiddle under your right arm and pluck the notes with the thumb of the right hand.

This is much easier because you do not have to have the fiddle continually under your chin in the playing position, and it is also quicker. You can give yourself a little rest and, of course, it looks interesting to see a fiddle player playing the fiddle as if it were a guitar or a banjo.

In the Elgar Violin Concerto there is a bit with a cadenza for the solo violin and part of it is accompanied by strings pizzicato in the guitar-banjo style so that you get a tremolo effect with the pizzicato.

You should practise pizzicato because to play it properly you must know exactly when the note is going to sound. In other words, you must put down the finger that you are going to pluck the string with and you must pluck it at exactly the time the note should sound.

# Use of the Mute

Certain pieces are written to be played muted and on the piece of music will be written 'Muted' or 'Con Sordini'; or 'Unmute' or 'Senza Sordini'. There are so many mutes that one can buy that it is impossible to tell anybody really what sort to buy. The best thing to do is to take you violin with you to a dealer and he will show you a selection and you can try them on the spot. See which you think gives you the nicest sound. All that happens is that you actually mute the sound.

Some mutes can be fitted on to the violin so that they are there all the time and you just slide it from the tailpiece down on to the bridge.

If you are playing a solo piece and there is a rather lovely melody which is repeated, you might play it the first time unmuted and then put the mute on for the repeat, which makes for rather a nice change. In this case you would not have 'Mute' on the music, you would just decide for yourself.

# Double-Stopping

Double-stopping means playing more than one note at a time. It is possible to play a three-note chord with the same bow, but usually it concerns two notes, usually either a sixth or a third — seldom a fifth because of the intonation difficulties. It should be noted that orchestral players are rarely asked to play two notes at the same time (double stopping). The notes will be divided amongst all the players in the appropriate string section. It is only as a soloist you might be called upon to play, in a certain piece, some double-stopping, a third, a sixth or even a fourth. And, of course, in chamber music and in a string quartet, there might be some double-stopping. A comprehensive guide to Double-Stopping is included in the scale section, starting on page 65.

# Harmonics

Natural harmonics are usually the harmonic on the open string, where you put your third finger down on the G string but don't press it down, keep it resting on top of the string and draw the bow in the normal way and you'll get a harmonic G. The same with the D string. These are the natural harmonics in the first position.

In the third position you get them by extending the fourth finger so that it is on G on the G string and that will sound G.

You can go to the top of the fiddle and get E, A, D and G natural harmonics, but then you are very high on the fiddle, almost to the top of the fingerboard.

An artificial harmonic is made by stopping the note with your first finger and resting the fourth finger on top of the string you are playing and you'll produce a harmonic which is one octave, or in some cases, two octaves higher than the note you have your finger on.

# Changing Broken Strings

There are different types of strings. G, D, A are what we call 'covered strings'. They have a gut core — or a steel one — and they are covered with thin spun wire. The most popular make is Pirastro.

One end of the string is knotted and that goes through a prepared hole in the tail piece for that particular string. This hole is a key-hole shape, that is, there is a little round hole and then a straight piece. You put the string in the round hole, so that the knot is underneath, and then pull it through the straight bit so that the string is held in place. You then take the string over and insert it into the correct peg — you can't put a D string into a G string peg — the holes in the tail piece correspond geometrically to the holes in the pegs — a pair of tweezers kept in your case, can be very useful to pull the string through, you then pull the string lengthwise. The other end of the string is beautifully wound and very thin and goes into the very small hole in the peg. Push it though as far as you can, pull it round a bit and turn it over on to the string itself so that when you tighten the peg you tighten the string. You should always look at a fiddle before you start to play and before you put it away, and there are a couple of things that can happen which will mean you have to change a string. You can see suddenly that a string has started to unwind, you'll see that a bit of the very thin wire winding has broken, and this means you have to change the string.

Also a string can break when you are playing or you can find one is broken when you open the case the next day after putting away apparently alright. You have to face the fact that a string can, and will, break while you are playing. The only recommendation I can make is that you always keep a couple of spares. Replace them, just as the efficient housewife always buys a replacement right away when she opens the last tin or jar of any commodity.

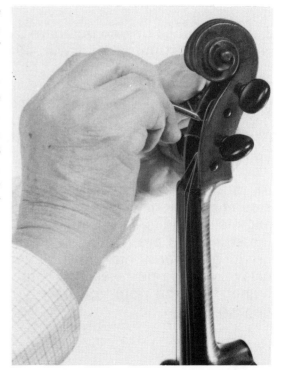

# Golden Rules

Keep the fingernails of your left hand trimmed so that the ball of each finger makes a good contact with the string.

You cannot make music with dirty hands.

Always keep your violin in its case.

After you have finished playing each time you'll find you have got a certain amount of rosin deposited on to the violin and you should always clean this away with a soft cloth while it is still in powder form and before it cakes. You should also clean the stick of the bow which will get rosin on it from the hair of the bow.

Before beginning a series of concerts I always take my violin in to be 'serviced' by an expert as things can go wrong inside the instrument which cannot be seen. Or, a violin can be 'open', that is, part of it can become unglued, perhaps where the hand is constantly rubbing against the violin in the third position. But, these are things which need not bother you at the beginning of your studies.

One of the most important things I would suggest to the student is to listen to violin playing on disc or radio. And I mean REALLY listen, especially if you can find a piece you happen to be particularly interested in and have the music for. Listen to the great players. I disagree with a lot of people who say it is a bad thing to copy. I feel it depends on who you are trying to copy. If you are trying to copy Jascha Heifetz I feel it is, perhaps, a little immodest of you to think you are good enough to copy him, but that is not the point. The point I am making is that if you copy that style, that beauty of expression, that phrasing, that clean technique — that is what you'll learn from listening to these great players. If they do a rather difficult piece of finger work in a certain way, at least you know it can be done and can think that maybe you will be able to do it too if you practise.

# Useful Musical Terms and Signs

To repeat a section of music, this sign 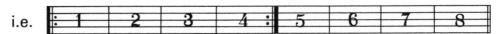 is used, and you repeat back to the bars shown between the two sets of dots.

i.e.

| 1 | 2 | 3 | 4 : | 5 | 6 | 7 | 8 |
|---|---|---|------|---|---|---|---|

In this you would play the bars in the following sequences, 1, 2, 3, 4, 1, 2, 3, 4, 5, 6, 7, 8.

1st & 2nd TIME BARS are also used and are shown thus:

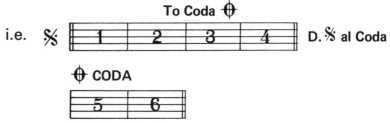

In this passage you would play Bars 1, 2, 3, 4, 1, 2, 3, 5 in that order.

Sometimes this sign ❧ is used, in which case you go on in the music until you come to the sign  D. ❧ al Coda ⊕   which means you go back to the sign ❧ and follow the music until you come to   ⊕ To Coda.   Here you go to the ⊕ CODA   which is found after the  D. ❧ al Coda.

To Coda ⊕

i.e.  ❧

| 1 | 2 | 3 | 4 |    D. ❧ al Coda |
|---|---|---|---|----------------|

⊕ CODA

| 5 | 6 |
|---|---|

In the above you would play bars 1, 2, 3, 4, and 1, 2, 3, 5, 6.
The letters D.C. mean go back to the beginning. FINE means finish.
8va over the stave means play one octave higher. Similarly 8va under the stave means play one octave lower.

Degrees of speed are shown as follows:—

| ANDANTE | Fairly slow, but flowing |
| ADAGIO | Slow |
| LENTO | Slow |
| MODERATO | Moderate |
| ALLEGRO | Quick |
| PRESTO | Quick |

Degrees of loudness and softness are shown by the following signs placed below the Stave:

| $pp$ | Very very soft |
| $p$ | Soft |
| $mf$ | Medium loud |
| $f$ | Loud |
| $ff$ | Very loud |

To speed up or slow down the following terms are used:

| RALLANTANDO | | |
| RALL | Slow Down | |
| RIT | | |
| RITARD | | |

| ACCEL | Go Quicker |
| ACCELERANDO | |

Pause  ⌢     Accent  >  ∧

# Tunes to Play

## First Position

## Third Position

## First and Third Positions

## Double Stopping

## First Position

**The Ash Grove**

**Drink To Me Only**

## Beautiful Dreamer

## The Keel Row

## The Oak And The Ash

# Third Position

### Robin Adair

### Golden Slumbers

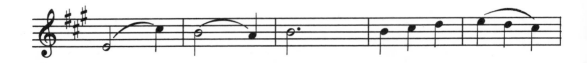

## When Johnny Comes Marching Home

## Amazing Grace

## Abide With Me

## The Last Rose Of Summer

# First and Third Positions

## Morning Has Broken

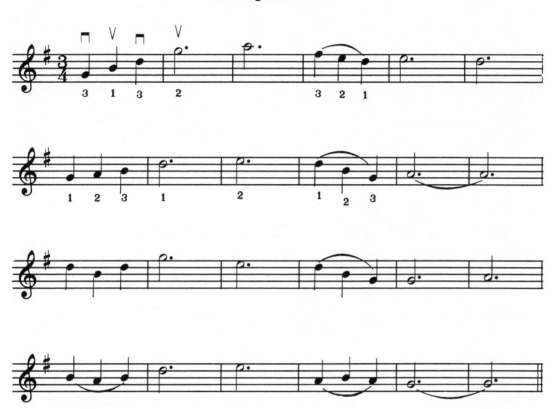

## Shenandoah

## My Grandfather's Clock

## Silent Night

## I Dream Of Jeannie With The Light Brown Hair

# Double Stopping

## The Camptown Races

## All Through The Night

# Scales and Arpeggios

So far the scales and arpeggios you have learned are all based in the first and third positions. However, for more fluent playing, the use of mixed positions are to be recommended as used in the following section.

## G Major

Scale

Arpeggio

Double Stopping — Thirds

Double Stopping — Sixths

## E Minor

Scale

Arpeggio

Double Stopping — Thirds

Double Stopping — Sixths

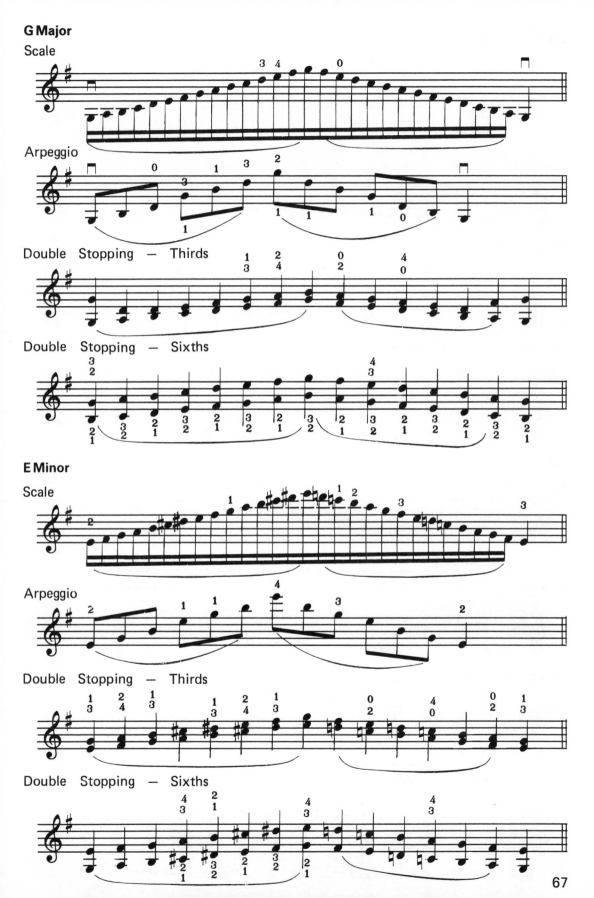

## D Major

Scale

Arpeggio

Double Stopping — Thirds

Double Stopping — Sixths

## B Minor

Scale

Arpeggio

Double Stopping — Thirds

Double Stopping — Sixths

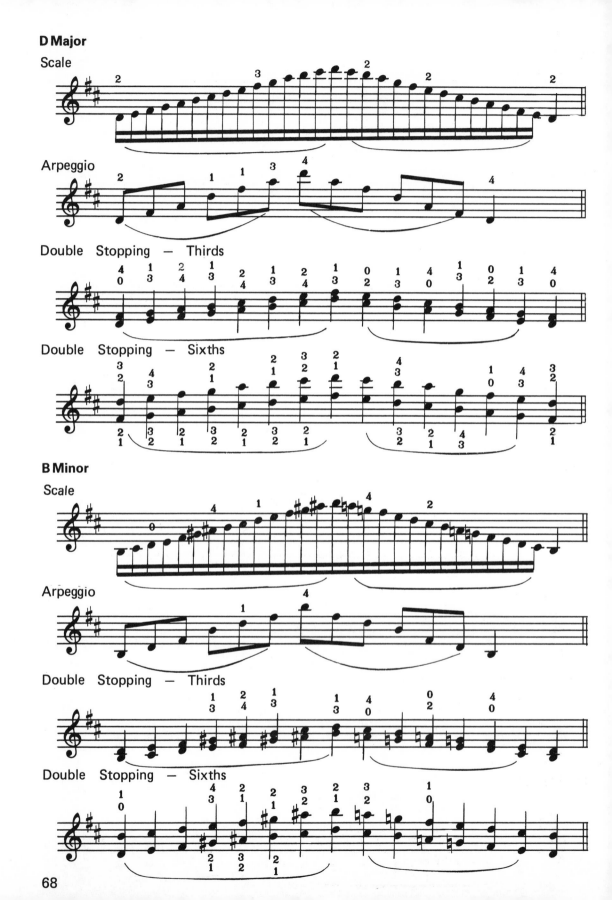

## A Major

### Scale

### Arpeggio

### Double Stopping — Thirds

### Double Stopping — Sixths

## F♯ Minor

### Scale

### Arpeggio

### Double Stopping — Thirds

### Double Stopping — Sixths

## E Major

Scale

Arpeggio

Double Stopping — Thirds

Double Stopping — Sixths

## C# Minor

Scale

Arpeggio

Double Stopping — Thirds

Double Stopping — Sixths

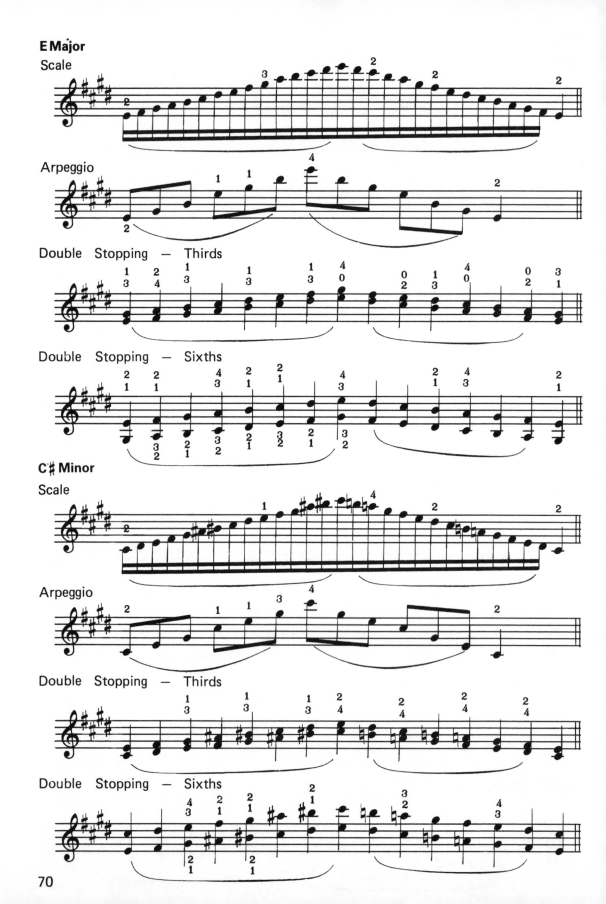

## B Major

**Scale**

**Arpeggio**

**Double Stopping — Thirds**

**Double Stopping — Sixths**

## G# Minor

**Scale**

**Arpeggio**

**Double Stopping — Thirds**

**Double Stopping — Sixths**

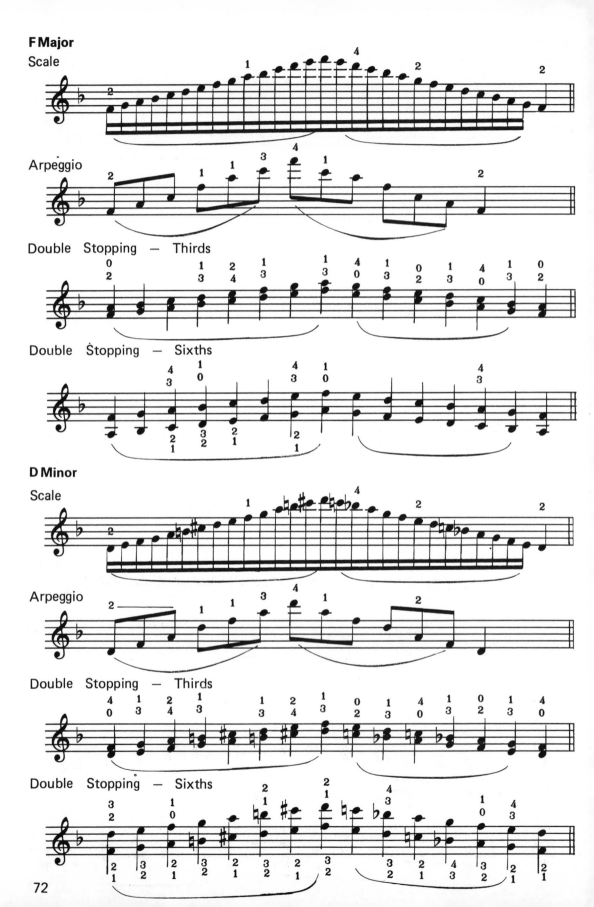

**F Major**

Scale

Arpeggio

Double   Stopping   —   Thirds

Double   Stopping   —   Sixths

**D Minor**

Scale

Arpeggio

Double   Stopping   —   Thirds

Double   Stopping   —   Sixths

**B♭ Major**

Scale

Arpeggio

Double   Stopping   —   Thirds

Double   Stopping   —   Sixths

**G Minor**

Scale

Arpeggio

Double   Stopping   —   Thirds

Double   Stopping   —   Sixths

73

## E♭ Major

**Scale**

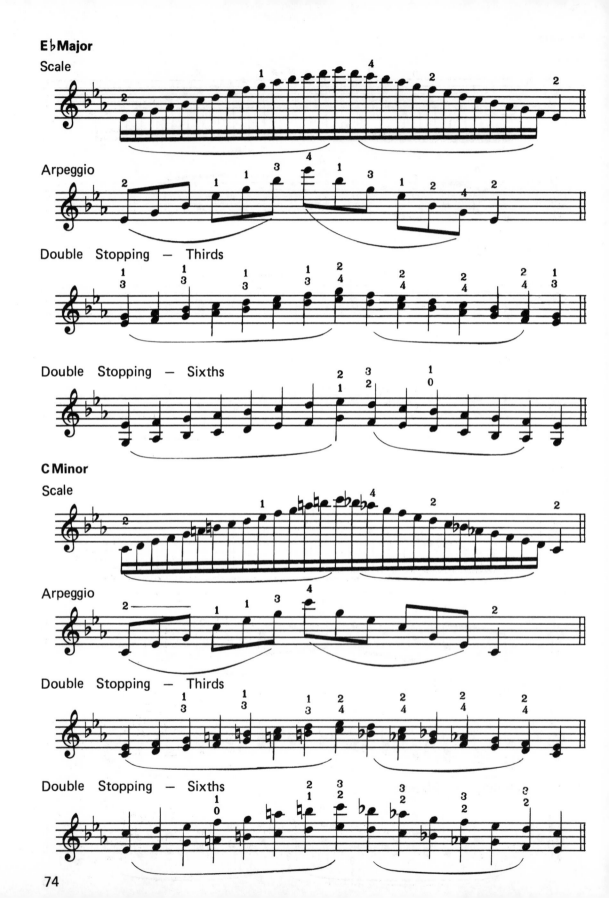

**Arpeggio**

**Double Stopping — Thirds**

**Double Stopping — Sixths**

## C Minor

**Scale**

**Arpeggio**

**Double Stopping — Thirds**

**Double Stopping — Sixths**

## A♭ Major

Scale

Arpeggio

Double Stopping — Thirds

Double Stopping — Sixths

## F Minor

Scale

Arpeggio

Double Stopping — Thirds

Double Stopping — Sixths

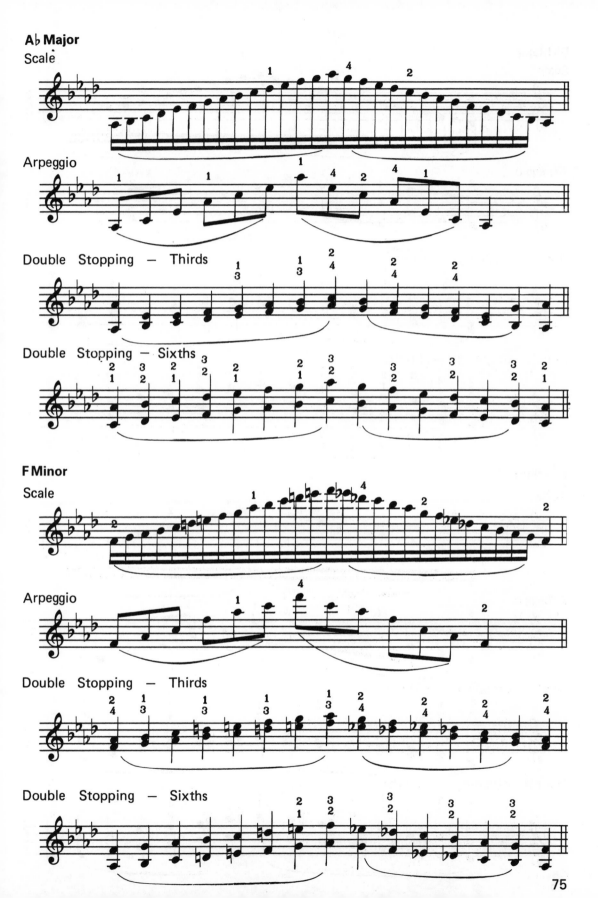

## D♭ Major

### Scale

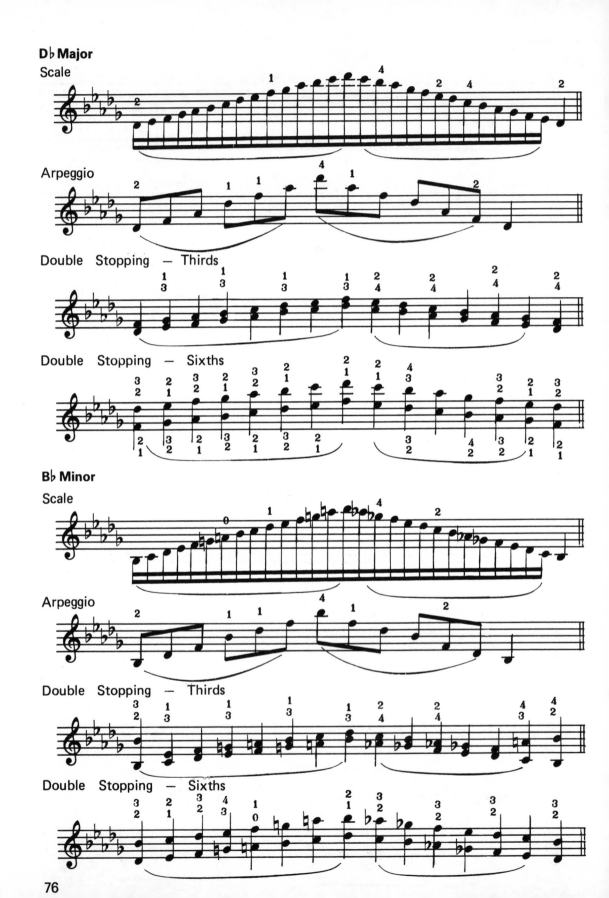

### Arpeggio

### Double Stopping — Thirds

### Double Stopping — Sixths

## B♭ Minor

### Scale

### Arpeggio

### Double Stopping — Thirds

### Double Stopping — Sixths

# Your First Repertoire

# The Skater's Waltz

**Waldteufel**

# Tango

Albeniz

79

# Largo

Handel

## Hedge Roses

Schubert

# Minuet In G

Beethoven

3rd Position

1st Position

Fine

D.C. al Fine

# Fur Elise

**Beethoven**

# Morgenblatter
### (Morning Papers)

Strauss

# Melody In F

Rubenstein

# Pizzicato

## (Sylvia)

Delibes

**Pizzicato Polka**

Moderato
pizz.

Strauss

87

# Habenera
## (Carmen)

dim. e rit.                a tempo

# Espana

Chabrier

# Dance Of The Sugar Plum Fairy

Tchaikovsky

**Moderato**

# Barcarolle
### (Tales Of Hoffman)

Offenbach

# To A Wild Rose

# Air On A G String

Bach

# Discography

The following is a small selection of records which I recommend for your further enjoyment and instruction.

**HEIFETZ, Jascha**
Beethoven, Piano Trios (exc)
Brahms, Violin Concerto
Mendelssohn, Violin Concerto Op 64
Tchaikovsky: Violin Concerto

**KREISLER, Fritz**
Concerto in the style of Vivaldi
Concert, O. Shumsky, M. Kaye

(LA) Gitana - violin & piano
Concert 2 discs F. Kreisler. F. Rupp

Leibeslied
Concert 2 discs F. Kreisler. F. Rupp

Rondino on a theme by Beethoven
Concert 2 discs F. Kresiler. F. Rupp

Variation on a theme by Corelli
Concert O. Shunsky. M. Kay (7/85) (ASV) ALH959 [4] ZCALH959

**MENUHIN, (Sir) Yehudi**
Bach : Brandenburg Concerti
        Suites, BWV 1066-9
Beethoven : Piano Trios
            Violin Concerto
Brahms : Double Conterto
Bruch : Violin Concerto 1

**OISTRAKH, David**
Bach and Vivaldi violin concertos 413 515-1 GXS (DG)

**PERLMAN, Ithzak**
Bartok : Violin concerto 2
Beethoven : Piano trios (exc)
Berg : Violin concerto
Bruch : Violin concerto 1
Khachaturian : Violin concerto
Kim : Violin concerto
Mendelssohn : Violin concerto Op. 64
Mozart : Concertone K.190
         Sinfonia Concertante K.364
Starer : Violin Concerto
Stravinsky : Violin Concerto
Tchaikovsky : Meditation, Op.42/1

**ZUKERMAN, Pinchas**
Beethoven : Violin sonata 5.
            Violin sonata 9.
Brahms : Violin concerto
         Violin sonata 2.
Mozart : Concertone K.190
         Sinfonia concertante K.364
Tchaikovsky : Piano trio Op.50
DC40158 [4] DCT 40158 (CBS)
Works for violin by Vivaldi, Wieniawski, Kabalevsky and Bloch

The following albums, recorded by Max Jaffa, available at the time of going to press, illustrate his long and continuing association with the best of light music.

(The Editor)

## PRELUDE TO ROMANCE
## MAX JAFFA — HIS VIOLIN AND ORCHESTRA

| | |
|---|---|
| PRELUDE TO ROMANCE | THE POET AND I |
| THE TOUCH OF YOUR LIPS | EASY TO LOVE |
| DON'T BLAME ME | I'M GETTING SENTIMENTAL OVER YOU |
| WHERE OR WHEN | LULLABY OF BIRDLAND |
| TRY A LITTLE TENDERNESS | MORE THAN YOU KNOW |
| YOU MADE ME LOVE YOU | I'LL SEE YOU IN MY DREAMS |

ALBUM > VAL.8051    CASSETTE > VAL.68051

## MAX JAFFA — MUSIC FOR A GRAND HOTEL

| | |
|---|---|
| ROSES FROM THE SOUTH | THE GREAT WALTZ SELECTION |
| SCARBOROUGH FAIR | CANTO AMOROSO |
| ADORATION | SOMEDAY I'LL FIND YOU |
| GYPSY CARNIVAL | DOBRA, DOBRA |
| I DREAM OF JEANNIE WITH THE LIGHT BROWN HAIR | FASCINATION |
| MEMORIES OF RICHARD TAUBER | VICTOR HERBERT SELECTION |

ALBUM > VAL.8057    CASSETTE > VAL.68057    COMPACT DISC > VALD.8057

## MAX JAFFA — GRAND HOTEL MEMORIES

| | |
|---|---|
| TIK TAK POLKA | HEYKENS SERENADE |
| INTERMEZZO FROM 'CAVALLERIA RUSTICANA' | DEARLY BELOVED |
| WHERE MY CARAVAN HAS RESTED | THE LARK IN THE CLEAR AIR |
| ROSES OF PICARDY | ROMANCE IN A. MINOR |
| CZARDAS | MY DEAREST DEAR |
| OLD ENGLISH AIRS | OLD FOLKS AT HOME |
| | ANDANTINO (MOON LIGHT AND ROSES) |
| | AN OLD VIOLIN |

ALBUM > VAL.8058    CASSETTE > VAL.68858    COMPACT DISC > VALD.8055

# Bibliography

Kreutzer — 42 studies
Hans Wesley — Scale Manual
How to read Music

GOLDEN HOURS SERIES BOOK 4
GOLDEN HOURS SERIES BOOK 10
JAZZ VIOLIN
STANDARD SERIES BOOK 3
TUNE A DAY (REPERTOIRE BOOK)
TWELVE TUNES FOR VIOLIN
VIOLIN FANCIES
VIOLIN SHOWCASE

# Position Chart

Although there are no frets on the violin, lines have been added to the chart to enable you to see easily the relative position of notes on the four strings and the various positions in which they may be found, and the normal fingering.

The alternative fingering is often useful when playing chromatically, us[ing] the sliding finger.

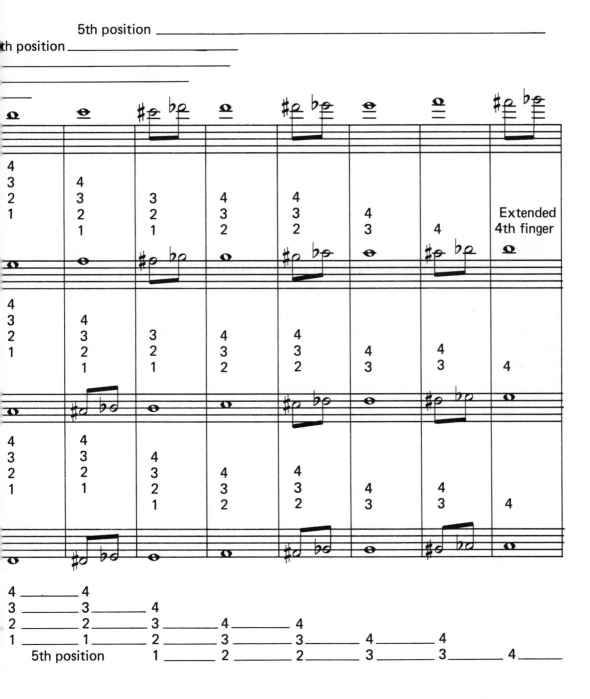

## "The best way to learn the violin is to play it"

To increase your interest and enjoyment in playing the violin, I would suggest that you experiment with alternative bowing and fingering. This will help with phrasing and changing positions and enable you to improve your performance.